PRACTICAL JOKES, TRICKS & GAGS

By Chris Tait

Illustration and Design: Willy Choi

PRACTICAL JOKES, TRICKS & GAGS

By Chris Tait

Illustration and Design: Willy Choi

Mud Puddle Books
NEW YORK

Practical Jokes, Tricks & Gags
By Chris Tate
Illustration and Design by Willy Choi

© 2010 by Mud Puddle Books

ISBN: 978-1-60311-101-0

Mud Puddle Books, Inc.
54 W. 21st Street
Suite 601
New York, NY 10010
info@mudpuddlebooks.com

Printed in China

Introduction:

The key to success with any great practical joke is simple and straightforward – the element of surprise.

Unless, of course, you can add in the element of an audience.
If you have both of these working in your favor, you've got yourself a humdinger.

I mean, a whoopee cushion on the seat is great for private pleasures, but a whoopee cushion in an auditorium before the assembly starts? Pure comedy magic.

So, before I begin to convey my infinite wisdom on the classics of the genre and on a few new tricky tricks, let me first say a couple of words of opening caution.

Practical jokes are not something everyone can pull off.

Oh, sure, you may think you're hilarious but some people may take offence and you may end up with more than you bargained for when it comes out that you've been the trickster behind said prank.

Because, as you may or may not know, the final and critical element of any great practical joke is to unveil yourself as said joker and to take full and entire credit for your great misdeeds.

Without the unveiling, practical jokes are just mishaps. How did that water fall on the head? Without the unveiling, it's never to be known.

Similarly, you can, in fact, over joke. That is to say, you can put yourself in a position where you are so obviously the dastard who does the deed that you are always in suspicion and therefore blamed for other's pranks.

It's a complicated world, kids. I just work the carnival wheel.

And finally, as a practical note, be always mindful of safety. Snapping chewing gum? Hilarious! Bed of broken glass? Emergency ward.

Its your call at the end of the day but I say safety first. Happy practical joking!

TABLE OF CONTENTS:

The Classic - Perched Pitcher

Oh, the perched pitcher. How I love its endlessly puerile gifts. You know, there's something about the simplicity of some practical jokes that just never stop giving.

The perched pitcher, I believe, was invented at exactly the same time as the door. It's my honest belief that someone finished leveling that door of doors and said, hey, check this out.

And their friend came over and swung it open and then swung it closed.

And then one said, so it just swings open like that when people walk underneath?

And the other said uh huh.

And then they both looked at each other and grinned like idiots.

Because they both knew what they were going to do.

splash!

Of course, we've all evolved since those early days and the first few fatal incidences with earthenware pitchers.

This is a wonderful April Fools gag for the family and one that any kid can be put up to or, frankly, if you have kids, blamed for.

It goes a little something like this.

First off, find yourself a door that you know will get heavy traffic in the morning. Now, you'll need to fully gauge the weight and width of your door and pick an appropriate vessel in which to carry your liquid reward but for me, I do like something a little larger than a simple glass, just for dramatic affect.

Of course, as noted in the earthenware trials, it's always best to use a plastic container of some description and to perch it just so. Too wobbly and you'll lose it before the gag goes down.

What you want is your unsuspecting prey to simply step through that door and whammo! Upturned pitcher on head.

It's really quite priceless and I recommend trying it on everyone in your family and possibly the neighborhood.

Small children, while blameable, may react by sulking. There's just no telling with the little people.

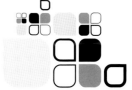

Mixed Nuts?

Now, of course, some practical jokes are not quite as old as perched pitcher but can still trace their pedigree to the times of Vaudevillian stage patter and the spritzer nozzles of yore.

One of these is the can o' mixed nuts. Mixed nuts are wonderful, as anyone can attest. So many choices, so many crunchy, salty delights. Who can resist? And of course, the answer is that nobody can.

And there in lies the beauty of this gag. For though the mixed nuts gag has been around forever, everyone, and I mean, everyone falls for it.

Is it because we're greedy? Is it because we're insatiable, forgetful, easily duped? I think it's just that we really like nuts and are ever optimistic, but that's your call.

To execute the mixed nuts, it's helpful to be in an environment where your said nuts are not going to raise undo attention. Parties are nice. Any social gathering will do. The lunchroom at work, even.

You'll want a few people to stand around and guffaw with you but you'll also want to be able to execute the gag a few times so don't be too showy about it. You'll have to decide in any crowd between audience and victim.

Next, simply offer your mixed nuts. Only you'll know that inside lurks that coiled spring of a snake and the joyful response that it will elicit.

Come to think of it, the whole nuts and snake thing is quite lewd. But enough of that, what we're here for is the response!

Depending on your level of cruelty or general viciousness, you'll want to decide between simply springing your nutty snake on someone who's simply standing quietly by or choose the bigger game of some-one involved in conversation.

I find these saps usually snap the loudest as they are distracted by talking and tend to shout out obscenities or nonsense, which is an added bonus.

Finally, it's your call if you want to go after people holding their drink. Will they spill it? Yes. Will they then spill it on you? To be discovered...

Psycho Shower

Now, here we start to move into the gags that require a bit more work and effort on your part but which are, in my humble opinion, quite worth the extra legwork.

I love this one because it's cheap (like me) and always elicits great energy from the participants (victims).

Now, I don't suggest that this is appropriate for the faint of heart, but it is a nice one for the older sister types and for those who simply could use a little lightening up.

If you are one of these types, please don't read any further as you will spoil what is no doubt being planned for you even as you read.

What you'll need – cherry Kool-Aid.

To set up your psycho shower, simply sneak yourself into the most used shower in your proximity. This trick works well for homes but can also be used for dorm rooms.

Next up, simply unscrew the nozzle of your local showerhead and sprinkle in a generous helping of your favorite brilliantly red colored Kool-Aid.

It's harmless, full of delicious empty calories, and, of course, best of all, really and truly will start any day off with a gory, gooey, terrorfest sure to make your smile brighter and your victim shriek in absolute fright before bursting into relieved laughter.

It's cheaper than a pot of coffee and just as effective to get the blood pumping.

Of course, this is just the kind of joke that elicits retaliation, so before you get too smug about it, here's another one, in the same room for you to watch out for!

The Covered Head

The covered head is less of a classic than it is a contemporary take on an old theme. As we all know, the burning bag of doggy doo on the doorstep has long since gone out of fashion, victim of a changing time along with the ascot and the two-step.

For today's youngster, there's the wonder of synthetics and of the joy of that miracle material – cellophane. Call it plastic wrap, call it shrink-wrap just don't call me late for dinner. That didn't quite pan out but you get the idea.

It's a simple material designed to keep in freshness and flavor. A technological advancement without which leftovers would be but a fond memory.

Oh science, you wanton mistress, what would we do without you.

At any rate, this gag is an inversion of the principle of the plastic wrap in that it's very purpose is not to keep in but to keep out. Follow me, if you will, down the rabbit hole.

AHHHHHHHHHH!

13

To execute this bathroom masterpiece, you will need a toilet, which I assume you have. Indoor, if you please. And you will need your trusty plastic wrap.

Now, here's what you're gonna do. Take your toilet seat, lift it up and beneath it, quite tightly place a nice taut film of cling wrap.

Now, as I mentioned, things are now starting to get a bit nasty and I assume this is a revenge gag for those who have had to endure the psycho shower or some other such bathroom mishap.

Now, the only issue with this gag, aside from the fact that it quite often ends in a little pee behind the knee, is that you don't get to see it go off. You'll hear about it. Oh, trust me, you'll hear about it.

But most likely, you won't see it going down and this a crying shame because it's equal parts, shock, self revulsion and then instantaneous rage that you really have to see to believe. How do I know? I too have been a victim of the covered head. And I too have lived to tell the tale.

Hooray for Whoopee

Now, as many of you know, the whoopee cushion is simply one of the most elegant of our modern creations.

Certainly, it resembles a cow's bladder and sounds like a pig's back end, but it does have its fetching qualities.

Namely, it is a lovely, powdery pink that goes with almost any complexion and décor and really compliments a family gathering unlike almost any other practical joke accessory.

Also, you'll find that its near universal appeal spans generational divides, cultural quagmires and language lapses like no other.

Wherever you are in the world, there is a whoopee cushion and there is not one among us who doesn't appreciates the squeaky, squishy, tooty, notes of its mournful and hilarious song.

And now, a few notes on its application.

SPLAB**ABAP!**
SPLAB**ABAP!**
SPLAB**ABAP!**

For me, the perfect whoopee cushion gag is about two things. The first among these is to pick the victim with great care. Is it funny if your big fat Uncle Carl lets out a big toot after he sits on your whoopee cushion?

Sure it is, but he does that anyway, all you've done is take the smell out of it for him. And what's the fun of that. Let him have his own finger pulling party on his own dime.

No, for me, I like to pick out the slender, clenched ones. The one with the finger up over the teacup. The ones with the pince-nez, the ones with the pursed lips. You know of whom I speak. These are your ideal target.

The ones least likely to let it rip in public and so all the more perfect to simply sit on the settee and squish in rippling harmony. And of course, once you've introduced your whoopee cushion at the party, you know it's the pastor who's going to borrow it next. I tell you they should give these things to peace makers the world over.

Lastly, it's about....timing. That's right. Lay your cushion in a loud and crowded room and you'll get a mild titter. A mousy chuckle perhaps from the few who've heard it.

Try it in a room where the silence has just begun or where someone is clearing their throat for their opening speech and now you have yourself a winner!

Slimed Handle

Now, while many of the jokes and practical applications here can be used once and then have you forever marked as a joker, there is a more subtle version of the practical joke that I might suggest to those with a little time on their hands.

These are the kind of jokes that are more like sociological experiments.

They give you the time to luxuriate in the glow of your ongoing prank and to wonder at the way that people's brains work and how they can possibly keep trying at something so simple.

To make this joke really sing, I suggest a cohort. Someone to sit with you and watch as an endless array of poor saps simply struggle through your slimed handle and make a mess of themselves.

What you'll need – Vaseline, and a good public toilet

Now, the slimed handle is simple because it's a simple idea: it's like watching a train wreck in slow motion for entertainment value. All you need to do is to apply a liberal dose of Vaseline to the selected door handle.

You'll find that your victims will spin their hands over and over around it. Think of the many times you've visited a public toilet on purpose.

Did you have to go a little or a lot? Was there a lot of clarity in your mind or were you simply reeling with the fact that you absolutely, without a doubt in the world, had to pee or die?

I suspect the latter and so you will feel some empathy with your victims as they twist and turn, clenching their knees and finally wrapping both hands in a double helix of frustration as they finally spring the door open and bolt inside.

And, of course, wonderfully, right behind them, comes the next mark, knock kneed and full of diet cola. It's a beautiful way to spend an afternoon and I suggest you bring refreshments.

Mixed nuts perhaps?

Shake, Rattle and Roll

What can be more sacred among human beings than the handshake? What other gesture imparts such a solid sense of moral connectedness and outright conviction and care for our fellow man? None, I tell you.

The handshake is the cornerstone of contract and of honest compact.

Now, how can we undermine this thing for good?

Ah yes, the hand buzzer.

The hand buzzer is a beautiful little contraption invented by Billy B. Buzzin in 1896. Billy was celebrated in his small town immediately after his invention—although sadly, within weeks—he had been hung.

It just became impossible to get anything done with these things kicking around and it was probably for the best.

But I digress. No, I won't hear a bad word said about the hand buzzer, deliverer of small jolts of friendly shock. It's compact, it's cruel and best of all, it's easy to conceal.

GZzzzzzt!

19

When it comes to the hand buzzer, I prefer —once again—to narrow the prey to a select group of individuals who love a big hearty squeeze.

The "put her there" fellahs. The ones who pump your arm like a shotgun and grin with every single one of their teeth clenched.

These are the manly men, the Miller men, the men for whom the hand buzzer was concocted.

I like to sidle on up to them, the strap of the buzzer on my middle finger, snugly out of sight as I offer up what I can only imagine to them looks like lunch.

The perfect, crushable, slightly effeminate hands of an author.

There for the taking. And take they do. And that's when they feel the full sting of electroshock shake ratcheting up their nervous system and sending them yowling.

The less advanced of the species often say things like "that's a helluva grip yah got there!" but most people know immediately that they've been had and they don't mind in the least.

They see it for what it is, a commentary on their massive shake and a good reminder that they are often crushing the life out of you.

Watch it when, after you've shown them how it works, and they've put it down on the table, when they reach out to congratulate your jest. Chances are you're gonna get the crushing of your life!

Black Out

Black Out is a great little parlor game but it requires a few participants to really help you out here as you perpetrate mischief on your fellow man. Now, the perfect scenario for Black Out is truly not the parlor itself but the great outdoors where you can gaze at the epic scenery.

You see, core to the gag of Black Out is the binocular. And, of course, to have binoculars, you must have something to "binocle." Something worth looking off into the distance and "oohing" and "aaahing" at. Now, you might try this on tourist relatives who've fallen into your care or you might opt instead for your actual nature enthusiast and lead them to the nearest waterfall/ravine/estuary, etc and then you may begin.

To enact Black Out, you'll need to have a set of binoculars and some art charcoal. We like art charcoal the best of all of the charcoals (Santa's, those from train tracks, etc) simply because it leaves a nice strong residue when pressed up against skin and leaves a lasting impression that is only minorly toxic. Minorly? Minorly.

So, once you've inked up your binoculars, you'll want to take your posse somewhere where they can almost see the cockatoos or hear the rushing torrent. Then you're free to offer up your binoculars.

Now, in any crowd, there will be those who strain to see what the binocular wearer is seeing and those who look at the binoculist to gauge their reaction. The latter are your immediate confidants as they will suddenly see what has been left behind on the face of the unsuspecting dupe.

Give them a wee nod and they'll be sure to chirp in.

"Jan," they'll say, "have you seen the amazing view? It really is stellar."

In this confusion, you can often net a few of your pals to look like Petey from our gang before the gig is up. Hopefully you're not with any serious bird watchers who will take offence. In my humble opinion, there are a lot worse ways to get yourself a nice new shiner!

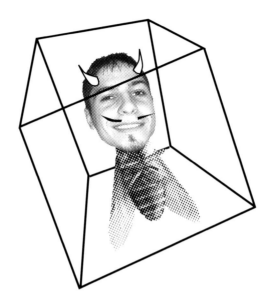

I fly with my little eye...

You know, it's a fairly well known fact that we humans will eat just about anything. I mean, we eat bark, roots, bugs, processed cheese even! The truth is we're walking trash compactors and we love it. Bring it on. Load it up. Sprinkle on some bacon bits and lets have it dipped in butter.

But there's something about North Americans and flies that is just outright hostile. We hate them. They repel us.

Certainly, they are repugnant little winged beasties but consider the way you feel about say, a caterpillar vs. your feelings for the common housefly.

One, cute, the other, to be slaughtered with the nearest issue of the *Times*.

Which is of course why the fly in the ice cube is an enduring practical joke for almost all dinner parties and social occasions. It's just flat out disgusting and makes for fantastic conversation.

I always think that it should be the host who puts the fly in the ice cube in the drink. It's a nice way to warm up a party and lets you have a little fun playacting.

Me, I always start out with disbelief.

I find that's a nice opener.

It's simply not possible, I protest.

Then, I move quickly to affronted.

Are you saying my house isn't clean?

And then, I move to indignant.

Well, if you think that's the kind of thing that I would serve to my guests perhaps this isn't the right place for you and your kind to be anyway?

It's only possible to maintain this arch persona for so long before caving into fits of hysterics at which point it's imperative to fish out the ice cube with a spoon and offer the next sucker a cocktail.

After all, it's your party and you'll fly if you want to.

Bloody Knuckle

Now, many of you know the game of the same name which is bloody knuckles. This is a Neanderthal amusement in which you basically take turns rapping each other on the knuckles while the your opponent tries to move as quickly as possible out of your way. It's ridiculous if you ask me and really, nobody screams very much, which is always disappointing.

The bloody knuckle I prefer is a simple trick that has enjoyed great success the globe over in its simplicity and frankly, it's grossiosity.

Here's how to begin. First off, you'll need an empty ring box or other small container that you can make a small hole in the bottom of.

You're going to want to make a hole big enough to put your middle finger through and lay flat. Then, you're going to want to make sure you have enough cotton or batten of some sort that a ring might lay on to surround your mummified treasure.

Next up, you'll want to give yourself a little bloody flair, so make sure to take some red marker or paint and really give yourself a little gore to surround your treasure.

You should be able to slip your finger right in there and lay it flat and hold it in your hand as if you are about to show it to someone without it seeming awkward.

Now, the next section of this joke is really and truly up to your discretion.

Clearly, the objective here is to offer the box to someone, have them slip off the lid, see the dismembered finger, feel disgust and fascination and then the rest is up to you.

Do you, for instance, now wiggle the finger or jolt it straight upright to encourage the best response.

Do you lay it still and tell the victim to touch at which point you spring the finger? It's really a question of taste. As is the final touch to this macabre little trick.

If you are brave of heart and secure in your relationships, you may even wish to try this trick on your sweetheart.

Now, here's where the complication comes in. They will most certainly think you are about to unveil jewelry and perhaps even THE ring. If you think your relationship can withstand this joke, then I encourage you to try.

If, on the other hand, you think it's 50/50, I would back away slowly. Perhaps she would enjoy a hand buzzer more?

EE**E**E**k!**

Finger Trap

Now, here's one that dates back literally thousands of years. The finger trap is a favored Chinese concoction and one that I love for a variety of reasons. So get ready for some serious fun.

This trick is especially effective on the curious and on the young. It arouses instant panic and confusion and is a helluva good time, in my opinion.

It should be noted that finger traps are not dangerous, unless of course you are a pickpocket and merely using this trick as a setup for more nefarious pursuits.

At any rate, the real key to the finger trap is to ensure that your victims are literally in with both hands and that they are curious and pliable.

Get ready to set some traps!

Now, when you're showing someone the finger trap, one of the nice things about its construction is that it looks fairly innocuous.
It could be part of some party favor or a whistle. There's nothing ominous or outright dangerous looking about it.

In fact, its strength comes from the way the bamboo is woven together and the way that it coils over skin.

So, when you have your victim ready, tell him/her you about to show him/her a marvelous trick.

The key, once again, is to ensure that he/she inserts both fingers.

You'll notice that there is an opening at either end of your finger trap. Simply tell your mark that he/she has to insert an index finger into each hole.

Now ask him/her to pull with all of his/her might to get free.
It is quite literally impossible, for even the strongest of the strong.

When you're ready to release your victim, of course, you can unveil the last secret of the finger trap. This is, of course, that the release on these devils is not to pull but to push.

By pushing your index fingers inward, you widen the bamboo and you can then release your fingers one at a time. It's fascinating, it's simple and it's something that everyone will want to try to see if they can be the one to break the magic.

Holding Tank

One of the simplest and most effective practical jokes I know of is really a set up to a magic trick that doesn't exist. Here's how it works.

When you have an audience, again, or just have a room full of gullible folk, let slip that you know some magic you picked up from a "traveler" or some other shady type.

It's the kind of thing that people can't resist hearing about and you'll of course, have to oblige and show your pals.

But resist if you can, as long as you can. I find stalling, guffawing and generally claiming oh, I couldn't possibly will get some unlucky sap to insist that you show them.

Well, of course, you'll have to acquiesce. Who are you to deny the people their due?

Huh?

Now, the holding tank is in fact no magic trick at all but a simple practical joke that will leave your pals in stitches. But the build up is important.

First off, you'll have to tell them that it is in fact, an escape trick. But make it seem like you are the one who is going to do the escaping. To make your trick possible, you'll need an assistant and two glasses of water.

Now, you tell the audience, this is a magic trick long shrouded in mystery. A trap from which escape is almost impossible. First, I'll need to give my assistant these two glasses of water.

Now, get your assistant to hold out his/her palms face up. Next, place a glass of water on each palm and get him/her to concentrate on holding them very still.

Now, with casual elegance, sit down.

Remember, timing is everything. Your audience and your assistant will suddenly realize that they are absolutely stuck holding the bag. The room will erupt with peels of laughter and there will be nothing to do but watch as your poor mark struggles to escape without making an absolute mess.

It's your choice whether you let him/her squirm or jump in to save the day. Either way, try to be encouraging. Karma has a nasty way of coming back to haunt you!

Trick Gum

Trick gum is so nasty and wonderful that I think there should be a separate book just to detail it's many flavors and wonderments.

What greater joy is there than to give someone you really and truly love, something that you know they will gobble like a fiend and then go bug eyed in horror over?

Honestly, it's moments like these that make it worth getting out of bed in the morning and writing books like this.

Just remember, as with any edible trick, you run the risk of being spat at, licked and generally goobered upon.

These are occupational hazards of the practical joker and once again, I cannot suggest strongly enough how important hygiene is. If you're going to pull this stunt, make sure its on someone who's spit you don't mind.

GAHHH!

Now as I've noted, trick gum comes in many flavors and colors.

You may use the pack of gum that in fact shocks. This is an old favorite and variation on the hand buzzer.

A simple stick of gum is proffered and when the victim takes a stick, they find they have in fact been charged in a way that is shocking and disturbing.

Look forward to being slapped and probably, in all likelihood, chased down the block. People are odd about having a gift shock them and they will be sure to let you know their true feelings.

Good sports will ask to borrow the gum and try it on their own unsuspecting herd.

Other wondrous variations on this joyful pastime include pepper gum, which is both vile and treacherous and Blue Mouth, which is a gum that stains not only the tongue but the lips and teeth a vibrant and unforgettable blue that takes most of the day to dissipate.

Ah, the many ways in which we spend our precious time. What makes us love these jokes so? Something to chew on, isn't it?

Foam Alone

Now, the foam alone is a joke that finds its origins in the mess halls of private schools, training camps and in college lunchrooms across the country. Its beauty is that it not only has spectacular results but that it uses basic science that you might in fact one day use. I'm not sure how you might use it, but it works on real science type stuff and that makes it a joy to perform and observe.

Now, first off, what you'll need is an ordinary salt shaker that you can gain access to before anyone else enters the room.

Pry off the lid and empty the salt from the container. Now, fill, the container with the regular concentrated lemon juice you'll find just about anywhere. Next up, you're going to have to act a bit gingerly if you want your stunt to come off correctly.

You're going to need to place a thin piece of toilet paper or tissue over the opening of the salt shaker and poke it down to make a deep impression that will have some holding power.

Now, you're going fill that little hold with a teaspoon of baking soda.

Next up, you'll want to cover over this little contraption with a piece of scotch tape on the inside of the lid. This will allow your victims to have to give the good vigorous shake you're going to need to get your quality reaction.

Finally, replace the top of the container and trim off any excess tissue. You carry your little contraption to the table, being sure to keep it upright. Then get ready for some real fun.

The first person to shake the salt shaker will have to shake harder when they notice nothing is coming out. After they do, the tissue will break down and the acid base reaction will create pressure that should shoot the cap off and send a cascade of foam over the table with a lovely loud pop that should leave the room gasping.

It's amazing what a little chemistry can do for a simple lunch. Of course, you're probably going to end up buying someone a new lunch but pleasure does not come without its price and you're sure to be applauded and lauded. Or possibly tarred and feathered. I don't know your friends that well.

Funky Teeth

Now, we've all heard of the funky chicken and we've all danced the Macarena at a wedding somewhere but this is a great stunt that's really for the amusement of you and your friends where you don't know the intended marks.

All you need are some quality funky teeth. Now, these teeth are not meant be worn every day or eaten with per se and, in fact, if you show up and display them to your friends, you're likely to be told to stop being an ass.

That's why I recommend using them on absolute strangers who are bound by the laws of civility and politeness to give you the time of day.

It's an odd thing about us humans but we just simply can't help but engage and enmesh with people, no matter how they present to us and what they say. We're born suckers, everyone.

So, when you make use of your funky teeth, I encourage you to go all the way. Why not concoct an outfit that goes well with them. Me, I think the foam fronted baseball cap and checked shirt are a nice addition.

Also, accents can add to any disguise and so I would encourage a nice drawl and a kind of goofy inspired laugh were I you.

Finally, you'll want to approach the unsuspecting with some questions that are fairly obvious and that allow them to try and engage with you. Let your friends sit across the road as your mark tries desperately to give you directions without looking at your teeth.

If you're feeling extra brave, you might just ask them – do I have sumpin' in mah teeth?

Or possibly, you might also want to develop a slight hacking cough and finish your routine by actually spitting said teeth out on the street.

These are questions of flair and performance and I will leave them to your better judgment. But do show some panache and bite!

Vile and Bile

Now, if you are the type that doesn't like to see things that are disgusting, disturbing or, in fact, funny, then I encourage you now to turn your head away and leave at once. The following joke is not for the weak stomached or even for those who are prone to nausea. In fact, the purpose of this joke is to induce those feelings. Consider yourself warned.

Now, this is another of the great lunchroom tricks and gags that has been around at least since there have been hot water bottles—and probably even before.

To complete this trick, you will need several friends who will engage with you and who are good sports about this kind of thing. Also, who have the stomachs of iron so lacking in our youth of today.

First off, you're going to want to find yourself a good sturdy hot water bottle. Now, what you're going to do is to fill that water bottle with a goodly dose of pea soup. Pea soup you say? But that's insane. Trust in the wise, oh little one, and all shall be revealed.

ugh!

Next up, you're going take that water bottle and put it under your shirt. You can tape it to your chest, you can affix it to you undershirt, and it's up to you how you adhese it as long as it stays put.

Now, what you're going to do is go to the lunchroom, cafeteria or local eating place with your friends.

Yes, you are in fact going to do what you think I'm suggesting you do.

Sit down across from your friends. When you deem the time is right, start wretching and acting sick. Have them look concerned and worried and then, with a bit of gusto, lean over, hammer your hand to your chest and let fly.

The table will now be covered in what looks to be projectile but is in fact pea soup.

Next, act completely surprised and after a minute pause, have all of your friends grab their spoons and start eating away at the mess you've just made.

After seeming puzzled for just a moment, join in with them with your own spoon. The clever in the audience will have you pegged immediately. The rest will likely flee or make their own mess but this is really practical joke as performance art here and you must follow through and be brave for real affect!

Finger Nail

Now, the finger nail is another good one for parents and children alike as it combines elements of horror, gore and downright goofiness, all of which are just marvy if you ask me.

As with any practical joke, though the work is not in the propping but in the set up. So I encourage you to think of a nice, elaborate way to introduce your finger nail—or nail through the finger if we must be accurate.

To begin, I suggest that you set yourself up with some form of work project around that house that requires you to do a good deal of hammering and sawing and other types of physical activity. Remember, you've only got one really good chance to reveal the Finger Nail, so make it plausible and real.

Next up, get yourself out of view of your intended victim. You might try finding yourself a little corner in your workshop or your yard or just a place where you can be heard to be hammering away.

Now, you'll want to slip on your nail through finger and get ready. It's almost showtime.

If you have the energy, you should perform a nice loud hammering sound and then scream with all of your might.

This will bring your mark running to see if you are ok.

Be sure to conceal the hand with the nail through the finger behind the other.

Close your eyes and say – I can't look, is it bad? Which is irresistible to humans, for some reason.

No doubt they will say, show me.

And now you are ready for your big reveal. Enjoy your moment. It will be short lived and you will be called a long string of things you might find shocking. Again, that is, until the mark asks to borrow the finger to try on someone themselves. It's only human nature.

Free Money!

Now, there's nothing wrong with wanting money. I mean, really, it's what makes us do some of the jobs we've had to endure and how we pay for the things we need.

But it's also completely fascinating what people will do to get money that is really not of much use to them.

Take for instance, the lowly quarter. Now, the quarter these days won't buy you a cup of coffee, a hot meal or a cot. Those days are long gone.

In fact, a quarter might not even get you a piece of gum. I'm not really sure anymore what it's good for except that it's a form of measurement and a fraction and makes a friendly jingle in your pocket.

But all that aside, you'd be shocked what people will do to pick one up off the street.

Again, this is where practical joking falls into the realm of the sociological experiment and, as I always like to say, humans are more fun to watch than a pack of monkeys.

So, here's how Free Money works. Get yourself a shiny quarter. If you don't have a shiny one, shine one, it's easy and you can use your shirt sleeve. Next, find yourself a well worn and busy bit of sidewalk.

Apply some crazy glue to your quarter. Now, simply put your quarter glue side down on the street and stand on it for two to three minutes. It should hold nice and solidly and you are now ready to sit back and enjoy. Get yourself a cup of coffee, if you like.

Watch as almost half the people who pass buy stoop to pick up the quarter. That in itself is fascinating. But watch as more than half of those try again and again to pick it up. Some will kick it.

Some will even pry at it with their car key. It's amazing to watch and provides some real entertainment. And you know what, it just goes to show that you can still actually get something for the lowly quarter!

Where's it at?

Most practical jokes take place in a very short time. You set it up. You let it off. You watch for the reaction. Others are more of a slow burn and need time and deliberate intent for the true reaction.

I like to do this one in succession where I start nice and small and build up to something truly befuddling and bizarre. Here's how it's done.

It helps if you have a roommate in your dorm or a brother or sister or other family acquaintance that you can torture with this one as you will slowly drive them up the wall. And after all, that's what friends and family are for.

To begin, while your mark is out of the house, dorm or lodging, simply move a few of their books or belongings around. Nothing too extraordinary, simply reorder a few things.

This will make them feel a bit lost when they return but they'll put it down to nothing other then their own disorganization or a possibly strange moment in the fabric of time and they will move on.

Hmmm.

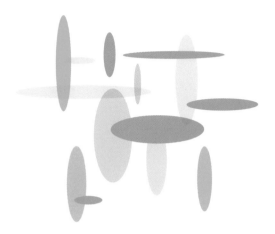

Next up, however, in a few days, you'll want to step up the routine. Shift a piece of furniture just a little to the left. Exchange a chair for another.

Again, nothing too drastic just enough to make them think they're starting to lose it.

Finally, within a few days, you'll want to pull the big finale. For this, I recommend getting yourself an hour alone with the contents of a room to really make an impact.

Now it's time for the big switcheroo. Move the desk to another wall. Put the bed somewhere else. Change all of the art on the wall to different locations. Take the books and rearrange them in backwards order. Really go to town.

This is essentially when your prey will suddenly realize that they are not going insane but have been had. They will certainly be hunting you in the halls but they will more than likely be relieved to know they will not be wearing the padded jacket any time soon.

Of course, you'll be gracious and offer your hand in helping to reverse arrange the joint. After all, it's only nice for you to restore furniture along with the sanity you've put in question.

Latherless Soap

I don't know who invented the latherless soap gag, but I would like to personally thank them for the hours of enjoyment they have wrought.

Again, as with all the best practical jokes, you need only simple ingredients that you can pick up almost anywhere and you are good to go.

To begin, you'll need access again to that holiest of all temples – the bathroom. Here, you will perpetrate your magic finale but first – to the preparations.

Find out what brand of soap your co-lodger uses. You're hoping here for someone who uses a simple brand of bar soap. If they use some hoity-toity salon brand of liquid so and so, you're probably out of luck.

What you're going to want to do is to take that brick of cleanliness and to coat it with a nice clear coat of nail polish.

Now, for those of you new to this kind of trick, it's really not that hard, even if you've never worked with nail polish, you can just apply as you would with a paint brush.

Now, what you're going to want to do is to let the thing sit somewhere where it gets good and hard.

You want this to be a cake of impregnability, one that drives the user insane when he/she tries to put it to good use.

Think of the moment when you are completely soaking in the shower and you reach for that soap and you apply it to your underarm.

You expect sudsy results on the double quick. And if you didn't get them, why you'd just rub harder, and harder.

That is, of course, until you looked down at that bar of soap and realized that it seemed oddly shiny. That there was something just a little off about it. And that would be when you realized you'd been had.

And you'd spring from the bathroom to wreak your revenge. And, if the joker was any good, that's when the perched pitcher would fall from the door top!